25 Important Questions

for

Mormons

Compiled by
Wilbur Lingle and Robert Delancy

PUBLICATIONS
Fort Washington, PA 19034

Published by CLC ❖ Publications

U.S.A.
P.O. Box 1449, Fort Washington, PA 19034

GREAT BRITAIN
51 The Dean, Alresford, Hants. SO24 9BJ

AUSTRALIA
P.O. Box 2299, Strathpine, QLD 4500

NEW ZEALAND
10 MacArthur Street, Feilding

ISBN 978-0-87508-539-5

Copyright © 2007
Wilbur Lingle and Robert Delancy

This printing 2007

Printed in Colombia

25 *Important Questions*

for

Mormons

What do you know about the Church of Jesus Christ of Latter-day Saints?

Perhaps a pair of young, smiling, conservatively dressed Mormon missionaries have been canvassing your neighborhood, aiming to "spread the gospel." They may have called at your door and offered to return and show you and your family a series of videos explaining why and how Joseph Smith was commissioned by God to "restore the true church," etc. Maybe they have given you a copy of *The Book of Mormon*, which is subtitled *Another Testament of Jesus Christ*.

Has your interest been aroused? Have you perhaps started a series of studies with these visitors, letting them explain their faith and why you should become a Mormon?

"Look Before You Leap" is a worthy adage, especially in religion. Before you go further and commit yourself, would it not be advisable to dig a bit beneath the surface? Have you read *The Book of Mormon* you were given? Have the missionaries let you see a copy of *Doctrine and Covenants* or *Pearl of Great Price*, two more books which they accept as holy scripture? Here are a number of questions you ought to ask both yourself and your visitors.

1   Did Ancient Israelites Colonize Large Parts of America?

The Book of Mormon opens with the account of an Israelite prophet, Lehi, in about 600 B.C, being warned by the Lord to take his family and depart from Jerusalem. After a lengthy and tumultuous journey through the vast Arabian desert, this extended family built a sturdy ship and sailed from its southern coast to their "promised land," America. Shortly after their arrival here they divided into two distinct groups, called Nephites (followers of Nephi) and Lamanites (followers of Laman). Laman and his followers rebelled against the Lord and so were cursed by

Him, resulting in the penalty of darkened skin. Hatred and constant warfare prevailed between these two nations, eventually ending with the extermination of the righteous, lighter-skinned Nephites, in about 400 A.D.—so states *The Book of Mormon*. (This, supposedly, is why Columbus found only dark-skinned Native Americans when he came to the New World about 1,100 years later.)

During the 1000 years that these two peoples coexisted they are said to have populated most of Central America and southern Mexico. They built and fortified many great cities, constructed temples and synagogues (Alma 16:13), built houses of cement (Helaman 3:7–14), established vast armies which used steel swords, breastplates and shields (Helaman 1:14–20), and even had horse-drawn chariots (Alma 18:9–10). They used gold and silver coins in their business transactions (Alma 11:1–20). They also kept extensive records of their national history, speaking and writing in both Hebrew and reformed Egyptian (Mormon 9:32–33).

QUESTION: If *The Book of Mormon* is accurate history and not just fiction, how is it that archaeologists have discovered *no ruins* or *arti-*

facts to substantiate these claims? No coins have ever been found, despite two centuries of digging. No iron or steel objects have ever been found. No swords or shields. No structures built of cement. No inscriptions written in Hebrew or Egyptian. And until the Spaniards arrived, horses were unknown in our hemisphere. The wheel was also unknown—hence no chariots.

There were Native Americans who *did* live in cities—the Mayas of Central America, for instance. Their remarkable civilization began in 3114 B.C. and did not crumble until late in the 9th century A.D. Linguists have now deciphered their 800 hieroglyphic signs and can study their extensive annals and their amazingly accurate calendar. *How is it that the Nephites and Lamanites never met the Mayas?* Is it proper for Mormon educators to disregard the Mayas' 4000-year recorded history?

2   Does Anthropology Verify Mormon Claims?

Anthropologists tell us that there are over 1,500 Native American languages. Ethnologists who have analyzed and compared the vocabularies and structures of these languages declare that not one of them even *remotely* resembles Hebrew or Egyptian—the languages of the Lamanites and the Nephites, according to Joseph Smith's book. Furthermore, the American Indians are racially *Mongoloid*, not Semitic, as DNA evidence conclusively proves.

QUESTION: Why does the LDS Church disregard these scientific facts?

3   Does Arabian Geography Match Nephi's Story?

Let us now consider some other strange details of this 600 B.C. migration. We are told in the second chapter of 1 Nephi, in *The Book of Mormon*, that the prophet Lehi (mentioned nowhere in the Bible), in order to avoid capture by the Babylonians, withdrew his family from Jerusalem. The account reads as follows:

> And it came to pass that he departed into the wilderness. And he left his house, and the land of his inheritance, and his gold, and his silver, and his precious things, and took nothing with him, save it were his family, and provisions, and tents, and departed into the wilderness.
> And he came down by the borders near the shore of the Red Sea; and he traveled in the wilderness in the borders which are nearer the Red Sea; and he

did travel in the wilderness with his family, which consisted of my mother, Sariah, and my elder brothers, who were Laman, Lemuel, and Sam.

And it came to pass that when he had traveled three days in the wilderness, he pitched his tent in the valley by the side of a river of water.

And it came to pass that he built an altar of stones, and made an offering unto the Lord, and gave thanks unto the Lord our God.

And it came to pass that he called the name of the river, Laman, and it emptied into the Red Sea; and the valley was in the borders near the mouth thereof. (1 Nephi 2:4–8)

These people were traveling on foot, likely using ox carts or donkeys to carry their luggage. Three days after reaching the Red Sea, they would still be on the coast of the Gulf of Aqaba, in the Midian Desert. But there are *no rivers* in that region! In fact, no rivers run into the Red Sea *anywhere* along the western coast of Arabia. Furthermore, as we read on, in chapters 16 and 17 of 1 Nephi we are told that they traveled southeastward across the empty Arabian Desert to the Indian Ocean. During this eight-year journey "we did live upon raw meat in the wilderness," and were guided by a "brass ball" which contained "two spindles" that acted as "pointers." Thus they arrived at "Bountiful," an unpopulated coastal mountainous region having much fruit, honey and timber—another geographical fantasy—where God commanded Nephi to build a sturdy ship for ocean travel.

QUESTION: Since the report of this journey conflicts entirely with the geography of the region, how is anyone to accept the account as fact? Forested Arabian mountains and wilderness riverbeds—if real—can't vanish without a trace, can they?

4   Did Jesus Visit Ancient America?

One section of *The Book of Mormon* (3 Nephi, chapters 9–28) describes the coming of the resurrected Jesus Christ to America in A.D. 34. It explains how Jesus taught the gospel and organized His church in the New World, introducing Christian baptism, the sacrament, the Lord's Prayer, etc. It claims that almost all the Nephites and Lamanites (the total population of the New World) eventually became converted to Christianity.

Equally astounding, Nephi tells us that 33 years earlier, after "a night with no darkness," that "a new star did appear"—the sign that Christ was born that day (1:19–21). "Now the Nephites began to reckon their time from this period when the sign was given, or from the coming of Christ" (2:8). So in the rest of this book, events in America are depicted as happening a certain number of years after this pivotal event.

QUESTION: Where is the evidence that any of the ancient American calendars—those of the Aztecs, Incas, Toltecs or Mayas—have any recognition of the birth of Christ? And where is one bit of evidence that Jesus came and converted anyone to Christianity?

5   Did Extensive Earthquakes Deform America?

3 Nephi 8:17–9:12 declares that at the time of the crucifixion of Christ, great earthquakes and other natural disasters occurred across America.

> And thus the face of the whole earth became deformed, because of the tempests, and the thunderings, and the lightnings, and the quaking of the earth. And behold, the rocks were rent in twain; they were broken up upon the face of the whole earth. . . . And it came to pass that there was thick darkness upon all the face of the land. . . . And it came to pass that it did last for the space of three days that there was no light seen. . . . And behold, the city of Gadiandi, and the city of

Gadiomnah, and the city of Jacob, and the city of Gimgimno, all these have I caused to be sunk, and made hills and valleys in the places thereof, and the inhabitants thereof have I buried up in the depths of the earth.

QUESTION: Where is the geological evidence that great changes took place in the American landscape as recently as 2000 years ago? And how could those three days of absolute darkness have been confined to our Western Hemisphere—for there is no mention of them in European or Asiatic records, much less the annals of the Mayas and other American peoples.

6 Is Ether's Chronicle about the Jaredites Believable?

Who were the *very first* inhabitants of the Americas and how did they get here? If one believes *The Book of Mormon*, these were the Jaredites, who established a flourishing civilization here and multiplied into the millions. All of them, however, were later utterly destroyed in a series of violent civil wars, fought with swords, shields and helmets of steel—the armies of Coriantumr versus the armies of Shiz—many centuries before the arrival of Lehi's family. All of this "history" is detailed in the book of Ether.

We are told that the Jaredites were originally a small family group who came to America soon after all other humans had their language confounded at the Tower of Babel. Ether's book recounts that these 24 men with their wives and children were commanded by the Lord to build eight small, airtight, dish-like "barges." Each of these windowless, submersible vessels had two small closeable holes, one in the top and one in the bottom (2:16–20). They were to pack these barges with adequate food and water for themselves and their flocks and herds (6:4). Then—despite the passengers' inability to build fires (2:23) or to open any hatches to expel manure—for 334 raw-food-only days (6:11) these unheated vessels were driven by never-ceasing winds halfway around the earth to the "promised land," America. Though these "barges" were "light upon the water," they were at times submerged "as a whale" and often were "buried in the depths of the sea." Though they had no sails, yet they were driven by "fierce winds"—and somehow all eight barges managed to keep close together for almost an entire year, until they landed.

QUESTION: How could enough food and fresh water for cattle, sheep, horses, asses and humans be stuffed into these "small" vessels for a trip of this length? Would not everyone have died of hunger and thirst, if not of agonizing seasickness or asphyxiation? Why were the Lord's instructions to Jared so outlandish and absurd?

7 Did Two Great Conflicts Occur in New York State?

According to the last chapter of the book of Ether, the final battle between the forces of Coriantumr and the forces of Shiz (rulers of the Jaredite kingdoms of Shule and Cohor) involved hundreds of thousands of people. Over two million mighty men and their families had been slain already (15:2). Now, "they were for the space of four years gathering together the people, that they might get all who were upon the face of the land" (15:14). Not just men, but everyone on the continent: "All gathered together, every one to the army which he would, with their wives and their children—both men, women and children being armed with weapons of war, having shields, and breastplates, and head-plates, and being clothed after the manner of war—they did march forth one against another to battle; and they fought all that day, and conquered not" (15:15). These pitched battles were repeated from dawn to dusk for seven days, leaving no one alive except Coriantumr and Shiz themselves; then one slew the other (15:32). This wiped out the Jaredite civilization!

Unbelievable as this is, there was a *repeat* of this battle over two thousand years later, when 230,000 Nephite warriors, plus their wives and children, were slain in battle by the vast armies of the Lamanites with their arrows, axes, and swords of fine steel (Mormon 6:1–15). And this occurred at the *very same place* as the previous clash of arms! In both wars, the contending forces had marched thousands of miles from their home cities in Central and South America, crossing the Mississippi and other mighty rivers, and journeyed through untracked land up to a small hill (Ramah/Cumorah) in what is now western New York State. (See Ether 15:11–12 and Mormon 6:1–15.) And, astoundingly, "Cumorah" is just about a mile from Joseph Smith's boyhood home in Manchester Township, N.Y.!

QUESTION: If these accounts are true history and not fiction, how do you explain the complete lack of archaeological evidence for these wars? Excavators should have uncovered hundreds of thousands of bronze tent pegs, steel

swords and axes, arrowheads and other imple-
ments at the battle sites. *Where are they?*

8 Is *The Book of Mormon* Worthy of Your Absolute Trust?

Despite all the historical and geographical er-
rors in *The Book of Mormon*—and we have noted
only a few—Joseph Smith described his *Book of
Mormon* as ". . . the most correct of any book on
earth . . ." (*History of The Church of Jesus Christ
of Latter-day Saints*, Vol. 4, p. 461).

QUESTION: Are you able to agree with that
assessment? Are you willing to stake your soul on
it? How much of *The Book of Mormon* have you
read? Can you conscientiously "testify" to its being accurate if you have not examined it with an
open mind? And have you ever compared today's
Book of Mormon with a copy of the original 1830
edition? You should! One examiner calls it "the
most corrected of any book on earth." Is a "burn-
ing in the bosom" (a "confirming" *feeling*) suffi-
cient evidence for believing this book of fiction?

9 When Did Joseph Smith's "First Vision" Occur?

The Church of Jesus Christ of Latter-day Saints was organized at Manchester, Ontario County, New York, in 1830 by a 24-year-old man named Joseph Smith, Jr., who claimed to be a latter-day prophet. He said that in the spring of 1820, when he was 14, "there was a great stirring of religious excitement among all the sects" in that region of New York State. Greatly disturbed, Joseph prayed to God, asking Him which church to join, and two personages appeared to him in a vision:

> I asked the personages who stood above me in the light, which of all the sects was right—and which I should join. I was answered that I should join none of them, for they were all wrong; and the Personage who addressed me said that all their creeds were an abomination in his sight. . . . (*Joseph Smith's Own Story*, printed in 1842, twenty-two years after it supposedly happened.)

Researchers, however, have uncovered solid evidence that in 1820–24 the churches of the area were actually losing members and that no revival meetings were held in Ontario County until the fall of 1824, when Joseph would have been nearly 19 years old! This dating places his "first vision" a year *after* the first visit from the angel Moroni (when, supposedly, the boy was first allowed to see the gold plates) which Joseph dates as September 21, 1823.

QUESTION: How can this discrepancy be explained? For an event of this importance, how could anyone miscalculate its occurrence by four years?

10 Who Appeared to Joseph, the Teenager, in His "First Vision"?

In his 1842 account Joseph Smith claimed that one of the personages who appeared to him in physical form pointed to the other and said, "This is My beloved Son, hear Him!"—so he saw both the Father and the Son! Many Mormons use this to try to prove their teaching that the Father has a physical body as well as the Son. But there are both *earlier* and *later* versions of this "first vision" account which vary greatly.

The first is a handwritten one by Joseph Smith himself, dating back to 1831 or 1832. It reads: ". . . I was filled with the spirit of god and the Lord and he spoke unto me saying . . . behold I am the Lord of glory. I was crucified for the world. . . ." (So this speaker was Jesus; no mention is made of the Father or any angels being there.)

Another account is found in *Joseph Smith's 1835–36 Diary* under the date of Nov. 9, 1835, when he was relating the first vision to a man named Joshua. Smith said, ". . . a personage appeared in the midst of this pillar of flame . . . another personage soon appeared like unto the first . . . and I saw many angels in this vision. . . ." (Now angels are introduced, plus the two personages.)

Then the *Deseret News* (an LDS newspaper) of May 29, 1852, under the heading "Life of Joseph Smith" quotes him as saying, "I received the visitation of angels. . . ." (Now no mention is made of the Father or the Son.)

Mormon leader Brigham Young in 1855 stated: "The Lord did not come with the armies of heaven, in power and great glory. . . . But he did send his angel to this obscure person, Joseph Smith jun., . . ." (*Journal of Discourses*, Vol. 2, page 167). (Now there is only *one* angel.)

QUESTION: Since all the above evidence, taken from authentic LDS material, indicates that the Father did *not* appear unto Joseph Smith, how can the present-day revised version of the "first vision" be proof that God has a physical body?

11 Did Anyone Really See or Handle the Gold Plates?

The gold plates from which Joseph Smith supposedly translated the Egyptian characters that became *The Book of Mormon* were never seen by anyone but *him*, for he kept them secreted in a box which he covered with a cloth. (Martin Harris, one of the supposed "Three Witnesses" to the gold plates, stated publicly that he had not seen the plates with his "naked eyes" but with his "spiritual eyes." He soon after left the Mormon church and joined the Shakers. The other two witnesses, Oliver Cowdery and David Whitmer, apostacized and were excommunicated a few years later.)

However, in *The Articles of Faith* by James Talmage (a Mormon apologist), pages 262–63, we have this description of the plates:

> The plates of *The Book of Mormon* as delivered by the angel Moroni to Joseph Smith, according to the description given by the latter-day prophet, were, as far as he knew, of gold, of uniform size, each about seven inches wide by eight inches long, and in thickness a little less than that of ordinary sheet tin. They were fastened together by three rings running through the plates near one edge; together they formed a book nearly six inches in thickness.

If we accept this description as accurate, what would the weight of the book be? Gold weighs over 1240 pounds per cubic foot; so a little calculating enables us to determine the book's weight: 234 pounds. But Joseph's mother describes Joseph as running with the plates for several miles and arriving at the house out of breath, but, strangely, without them under his arm, having deposited them somewhere (Lucy Mack Smith, *Biographical Sketches of Joseph Smith the Prophet*, pp. 104–5). What amazing strength!

Not only Joseph Smith, but the additional "Eight Witnesses" to the gold plates also exhibited rather unusual strength:

> And [to] this we bear record with words of soberness, that the said Smith has shown us, for we have seen and hefted, and know of a surety that the said Smith has got the plates of which we have spoken. (Introduction to *The Book of Mormon*, The Testimony of Eight Witnesses)

Just what Joseph Smith showed them we do not profess to know. He could have made a phony set of plates or something. But how many ordinary men of today could "heft" plates of gold weighing 234 pounds?

QUESTION: Are you willing to put your

trust in a fabricated book with a fabricated history when nobody reliable actually saw the gold plates—and it would have been impossible for anyone to lift or carry them?

In contrast to this, the Bible has a completely reliable and verifiable history. And the Bible solemnly warns against altering its message, even if an angel should be responsible:

"But though we, or an angel from heaven [Moroni?], preach any other gospel unto you than that which we have preached unto you, let him be accursed" (Galatians 1:8).

"And no marvel; for Satan himself is transformed into an angel of light . . ." (2 Corinthians 11:14).

12 How Was *The Book of Mormon* Translated?

David Whitmer, one of the "Three Witnesses," tells how Joseph Smith did his "translating." Smith never actually used the gold plates which the angel Moroni had finally, after a four-year wait, given to him. Rather, he simply used his multicolored, egg-shaped "seer stone" which he placed in his hat, and then put his face into the hat. A piece of parchment would appear, and on that appeared writing, one character at a time, and under it was the interpretation in English. Smith would read off the English to Oliver Cowdery, his principle scribe, who wrote it down and repeated it to Smith for verification. So the actual translation was by "the gift and power of God" and could never be changed—despite its poor sentence structure, bad grammar, and even contradictory statements.

(Both of these Mormon founding fathers, Whitmer and Cowdery, later on had a falling-out with Joseph Smith, were excommunicated, and were forced to flee for their lives.)

Even the typesetter, John H. Gilbert, was forbidden by Smith to change anything. This original 1830 edition of *The Book of Mormon* was claimed by Smith to be ". . . the most correct of any book on earth, and the keystone of our religion. . . ."

QUESTION: This being so, how do you justify the 3,913 changes—some of them quite major—made in later editions of *The Book of Mormon*? Which edition is to be believed? Why do most Mormons use the current *altered* edition rather than the original?

13 Could God Possibly Be a Racist?

Two drastic changes made in *The Book of Mormon* are these:

(1) The title page of the 1830 printing *accurately* reads:

BY JOSEPH SMITH, JUNIOR
AUTHOR AND PROPRIETOR

This has been changed to:

TRANSLATED BY JOSEPH SMITH, JUN.

(2) Nephi's prophecy regarding the complexion of the American Indians:

> And then shall [the Lamanites] rejoice; for they shall know that it is a blessing unto them from the hand of God; and their scales of darkness shall begin to fall from their eyes; and many generations shall not pass away among them, save they shall *be a pure* and delightsome [1830: *become a white* and delightsome] people. (2 Nephi 30:6)

This modification has helped the LDS Church evade longstanding charges of "racism." (During its first 150 years, blacks were almost wholly excluded from the privileges of temple endowment and from holding the Melchizedek priesthood. This was not revoked until June 1, 1978.)

However, Jacob 3:8 still reads: "O my brethren, I fear that unless ye shall repent of your sins that their skins will be whiter than yours, when ye shall be brought with them before the throne of God."

In line with this, Mormon writings teach that while each human was in the spirit world he went through a time of testing. If a person was obedient and valiant in the spirit world, he was assured of being born into a good family who lived in a powerful nation. If he was very good, he would be born into a white Mormon family. If he was less valiant, he would be born with darker skin, and the least valiant would be born with black skin. Bruce McConkie, Mormon apologist, writes:

> In the preexistent eternity various degrees of valiance and devotion to the truth were exhibited by different groups of our Father's spirit offspring. One-third of the spirit hosts of heaven came out in open rebellion and were cast out without bodies, becoming the devil and his angels. . . . Of the two-thirds who followed Christ, however, some were more valiant than others. . . . Those who were less valiant in preexistence and who thereby had certain spiritual restrictions imposed upon them during mortality are known to us as Negroes. Such spirits are sent to earth through the lineage of Cain, the mark put upon

him for his rebellion against God and his murder of Abel being a black skin (Moses 5:16–41; 7:8,12,22). Noah's son Ham married Egyptus, a descendant of Cain, thus preserving the Negro lineage through the flood (Abraham 1:20–27). (*Mormon Doctrine*, 1966 edition, pp. 526–27)

QUESTION: Do you believe this LDS teaching? Could God be a racist?

14   Has Mormon Doctrine Progressed or Regressed?

The Introduction to *The Book of Mormon* states: "*The Book of Mormon* is a volume of holy scripture comparable to the Bible. It is a record of God's dealings with the ancient inhabitants of the Americas and contains, as does the Bible, *the fulness of the everlasting gospel*. . . . It puts forth the doctrines of the gospel, outlines the plan of salvation, and tells men what they must do to gain peace in this life and eternal salvation in the life to come."

QUESTION #1: If this is true, why does the Mormon church believe in "progressive revelation"? Doesn't "fulness" mean "total" or "complete"?

QUESTION #2: If this "fulness" is a fact, then why doesn't *The Book of Mormon* contain any of these unique Mormon doctrines:

A. God is an exalted man with a body of flesh and bones and is the product of eternal progression.

B. God and His wives give birth to spiritual children through physical relations.

C. There are three heavens, and resurrected families can live together and continue to progress after leaving this life.

D. All humans preexisted before this earthly life.

E. Jesus was married; he had at least three wives and had children by them.

QUESTION #3: Why does much that is found in *The Book of Mormon* directly contradict what the LDS Church teaches today? For instance:

A. There is only one God (2 Nephi 31:21; Alma 11:26–29).

B. God is unchanging (Mormon 9:9–10, 19; Moroni 7:22, 8:18).

C. God is a spirit (Alma 18:24–28, 22:9–11).

D. We must be born from above to become new creatures; then we will have assurance of salvation (Mosiah 27:24–28; Alma 5:14–26).

E. We are to search the Bible to see if a religious teaching is correct or not (Jacob 7:23)—not just "pray about it."

15 Has Jesus Sanctioned New Mormon Doctrines?

In the eleventh chapter of 3 Nephi, Jesus is said to be speaking to the people of Nephi who are assembled at the temple in the land Bountiful.

> This is my doctrine, and it is the doctrine which the Father hath given me . . . and I bear record that the Father commandeth all men everywhere to repent and believe in me. And whoso believeth in me and is baptized, the same shall inherit the kingdom of God. (11:32–33)
>
> And whoso shall declare more or less than this, and establish it for my doctrine, the same cometh of evil, and is not built upon my rock; but he buildeth upon a sandy foundation, and the gates of hell stand open to receive such when the floods come and the winds blow upon them. (11:40)

QUESTION: Have not the prophets of the LDS Church established more doctrines than repentance, faith, and baptism? Have they not *added* temple endowments, sacred garments, eternal marriage, spirit children, family life on other planets, genealogical research, and the Word of Wisdom, to name just a few? According to 3 Nephi 11:40 these doctrines come from *evil* and "the gates of hell stand open to receive" those who teach such things. Does not The Church of Jesus Christ of Latter-day Saints stand condemned by its own book?

16   What Makes a True Mormon?

The LDS Church believes in "progressive revelation." All its presidents, past and present, are considered "prophets," and can receive new and binding revelations.

QUESTION: This being true, and since none of the above-mentioned esoteric Mormon doctrines are found anywhere in *The Book of Mormon*, then how could any of the Nephites and the Lamanites have been true Mormons? And yet they had "the fulness of the everlasting gospel," didn't they?

17   Was Joseph Smith a True Prophet of the Lord?

Joseph Smith claimed to be a prophet of the Lord. One of his most interesting prophecies, recorded in the official Mormon book *Doctrine and Covenants* (57:3), was made in July of 1831 while Smith and his followers were residing in western Missouri.

> Thus saith the Lord your God, if you will receive wisdom here is wisdom. Behold, the place which is called Independence is the center place; and a spot for the temple is lying westward, upon a lot which is not far from the court house.

And so, in Independence, Missouri, on August 3, 1831, eight Mormon elders assembled together at the plot where the temple was to be erected. Joseph Smith then laid a cornerstone, engraved with his initials and the date, at the northeast corner of the contemplated temple, and Sidney Rigdon pronounced the plot of ground wholly dedicated unto the Lord forever.

Smith taught that Jesus Christ would set up His millennial Kingdom there, and that all the nations would flow to it. He repeatedly prophesied that this temple would be built "in this generation" (*D&C* 84:4). He also prophesied that he would live until the Lord's coming to Zion. Yet he was killed in a "shoot out" at Carthage, Illinois, on June 27, 1844. The temple lot is now owned by a splinter denomination of Mormonism, with *no temple in sight*—and obviously all who heard Smith make this prophecy have passed away.

QUESTION: If Joseph Smith was a true prophet of the Lord, how could he have been so completely mistaken in this regard, for *not one part* of this prophecy has come true!

18 Did Joseph Smith Plagarize While Composing *The Book of Mormon*?

The separate books that comprise *The Book of Mormon*—supposedly engraved on the gold plates by 14 ancient authors and spanning 1000 years from 1 Nephi through Moroni—are stylistically identical! Monotonously so. Unlike the Bible—God's matchless, inspired Word—there is an obvious *sameness* throughout the whole. The favorite expression of these 14 scribes, occurring 1,272 times (but only 444 times in the whole Bible), is "It came to pass." This, along with "Yea, behold," "And behold," "But behold"—the repetition is astounding—produces a distinctly King James flavor. How could this have happened?

There is no question but that whole chapters of the Bible have been copied almost verbatim from the KJV. Chapters 2–14 of Isaiah in the KJV are largely identical to 2 Nephi, chapters 12–24, pages 81–96 in *The Book of Mormon*. Thousands of quotations from the KJV are to be found. In 3 Nephi, chapters 12–14, Jesus delivers to the Nephites a discourse similar to the Sermon on the Mount of Matthew 5–7, with only the slightest changes of wording.

The Book of Mormon also contains quotes from some of the books of the Apocrypha, and the 1769 revision of the King James Bible which Joseph Smith possessed included the Apocrypha.

Many of *The Book of Mormon*'s main characters were also extracted from the Bible, though names and circumstances have been changed to cover up this fact. Major portions of *The Book of Mormon* would be missing if all the direct quotes, indirect quotes, and references to incidents in the Bible were deleted from it.

QUESTION: Is it not obvious that Joseph Smith was the surreptitious *author* of *The Book of Mormon* and that he plagiarized drastically to compose it?

19 A Strange Sacramental Change — Is It Justified?

On the night before His crucifixion, Jesus met with the Twelve and instituted the memorial sacrament (eucharist) by taking two elements of the Jewish Passover meal, the bread and the wine, and declaring that they represented His body and His blood, which He was about to offer up on our behalf (see Matthew 26:26–29; Mark 14:22–24; Luke 22:14–20). In full agreement with this, *The Book of Mormon* states that the resurrected Christ commanded the righteous Nephites, in America, also to "break bread" and "drink of the cup of wine" (see 3 Nephi 18:1–3, 8–10; 20:4–9; Moroni 5:1–2), which they regularly did.

QUESTION: This being so, why do Mormons today partake of bread and *water* (not "the fruit of the vine") in remembrance of Jesus Christ's atoning sacrifice? Are we not to obey the Savior's specific commands? Why would God supposedly send a heavenly messenger to Joseph Smith (in August of 1830) to warn against the use of wine "of unassured purity" (*D&C*, chapter 27)? Yes, wine can be impure, but so can water.

20 Celestial Marriage — A Major Theological Problem

Mormons teach that people can live as families in the celestial kingdom. They hold that civil and church marriages are only for this life, but marriages performed or later solemnized in a Mormon temple will last for eternity. And the children of those couples are thereby sealed to them for all eternity.

> Marriages performed in the temples for time and eternity, by virtue of the sealing keys restored by Elijah, are called "celestial marriages." The participating parties become husband and wife in this mortal life, and if after their marriage they keep all the terms and conditions of this order of the priesthood, they continue on as husband and wife in the celestial kingdom of God. If the family unit continues, they by virtue of that fact, the members of the family, have gained eternal life (exaltation), the greatest of all the gifts of God, for by definition *exaltation consists in the continuation of the family unit* in eternity. (*Mormon Doctrine*, p. 117)

If this teaching is true it presents a major problem. When children get married, they start new families of their own. Mormon teaching is that each resurrected and exalted man can become a god and begin a *new* world with his wife or wives, and there beget, through physical relations, another generation of spirit children.

QUESTION: If parents' sons have the privilege of becoming gods with their own worlds and their own family units, then how can Mormon parents and children live together when they are in separate worlds?

21   **Eternal Progression —
          Preposterous!**

Mormons believe in a long succession of gods. They say, "What father didn't have a father!" To them, this settles the question—the process of becoming gods has been going on for many eons.

Milton R. Hunter, in *The Gospel Through the Ages* (pp. 114–15), states:

> We know that God absolutely transcends the finite understanding of mortals. . . . Yet, if we accept the great law of eternal progression, we must accept the fact that there was a time when Deity was much less powerful than He is today. Then how did He become glorified and exalted and attain His present status of Godhood? In the first place, aeons ago God undoubtedly took advantage of every opportunity to learn the laws of truth and as He became acquainted with each new verity He righteously obeyed it. From day to day He exerted His will vigorously, and as a result became thoroughly acquainted with the forces lying about Him. As He

gained more knowledge through persistent effort and continuous industry, as well as through absolute obedience, His understanding of the universal laws continued to become more complete. Thus He grew in experience and continued to grow until He attained the status of Godhood.

QUESTION: Where did this "law of eternal progression" have *its* origin? How could it possibly predate God Himself? If God gained more knowledge through obedience, *who* did He obey? Does not God declare, "Before me there was no God formed, neither shall there be after me" (Isaiah 43:10)? And did not Moses assert: "From everlasting to everlasting, thou art God" (Psalm 90:2)? If there is an ordaining intellect or "force" lying behind the Biblical God, should we not rather worship *it*?

22 A Contradictory Teaching about Jesus

The LDS Church teaches that it is absolutely necessary to have a physical body in order to start a person on the road to becoming a "god." In bold contradiction to this belief, it teaches also that Jesus was the Jehovah-God of the Old Testament.

QUESTION: How could Jesus be the Jehovah-God of the Old Testament when he was still in a spirit form and had not yet received an earthly body? According to Mormon theology, he hadn't even begun the process of becoming a god, let alone being the Mighty God who is revealed in the Bible (Isaiah 9:6).

23   Angelic Foolishness

Mormons speak a lot about the "ministry of angels," who are spirit beings. In fact, Mormon chronicler Bruce R. McConkie tells us that all "angels of the Almighty are chosen from among his offspring and are themselves pressing forward along the course of progression and salvation . . . because angels are of the same race as man and God" (*Mormon Doctrine*, pp. 35–37). The Bible also has a lot to say about angels, and many times they are classified as "holy" angels. It would seem that in their "first estate" (to use Mormon terminology) they were the "best" spirit beings. Mormons teach that the more valiant a spirit was in the preexistent state the better is its lot in *this* world! But we find that at the end of this world there are still holy angels who have never received a body so that they might work at becoming a god. There are a number of Bible passages which state that the *holy* angels will be the reapers at the end of the age (see Matthew 24:31 and 25:31; also Revelation 14:10). It seems that being a holy angel is a disadvantage!

QUESTION: Why, at the time of man's Final Judgment, will there still be holy spirits who have not progressed beyond angelhood?

24 Baptism for the Dead

Mormon doctrine insists that there is no salvation of the soul without faith in Christ, repentance, and baptism by immersion administered by a qualified Mormon priest. Mormons extend this obligation of baptism to everyone, including all who have lived and died without receiving a knowledge of the "restored gospel" as it was revealed to Joseph Smith. One of the most important works, therefore, that a sincere Mormon can perform is *proxy baptism* for one's ancestors and others of past ages who died without having this knowledge. Not that the dead person who is baptized vicariously is saved thereby, but that he will now have a chance, in

the spirit prison (hell), to hear and accept the
Mormon gospel! It is because of this doctrine
that Mormons today are so involved in genealogical research and temple work.

This doctrine is nowhere taught in *The Book
of Mormon.* (In fact, see Alma 34:32–34.) Rather,
it is based upon a misunderstanding of one verse
in the Bible. It is true that in order to support his
faith in the coming resurrection, the Apostle Paul
referred to some people who were being baptized
on behalf of their dead relatives: "Else what shall
they do which are baptized for the dead, if the
dead rise not at all? Why are they then baptized
for the dead?" (1 Corinthians 15:29). But note,
he did *not* say "Why are *we* then being baptized
for *our* dead?" No! He was talking about some
other people; evidently a Jewish sect with Gnos-
tic leanings had sprung up in the vicinity and
this was *their* practice.

Mormons also teach that Jesus preached the
gospel to the spirits of all the dead during the
three days between His crucifixion and resurrection. The repentant ones among these dead
therefore need, they say, to be baptized by proxy.
They use 1 Peter 3:19 as their proof text. But a
person should read the rest of the chapter, verses

20–22. Are we to infer that these imprisoned spirits who, while alive on earth, had "disobeyed" Noah's preaching for up to 120 years are given a second chance to repent? No; obviously they are not *innocent* people. So did Jesus visit these spirits as an evangelist or as a herald—and why did He go particularly to them? Not as an evangelist, for "it is appointed unto men once to die, but after this the judgment" (Hebrews 9:27). There is *no* "second chance" for personal salvation after death (read Luke 16:19–31). Rather, Jesus appeared and spoke to these *condemned* spirits in order to visibly affirm the truths preached to them earlier by Noah (2 Peter 2:5)—for in spurning Noah's ark for their physical salvation they had likewise spurned Him, the true Ark, who was provided for their *spiritual* salvation. Indeed, the one refuge from ruin prefigures the other.

The "condemned" earth (Hebrews 11:7) being "resurrected," so to speak, from the Flood is recognized by Peter to be a picture of water baptism, in which we show that we have been saved from death and doom by the resurrection of Christ (Romans 6:4). But, Peter declares, one's appealing to God for a "good conscience" (v. 21) is the *essential* element—any outward "putting away of the filth of the flesh" being otherwise of no consequence.

In short, water baptism does *not* give eternal life: Jesus Christ, the resurrected and ascended Savior, if trusted alone and fully, *does*! So, concerning the LDS doctrine of "baptism for the dead"—

QUESTION: Since "baptism for the dead" is such an important teaching, affecting millions of lives—and remember, Joseph Smith said *The Book of Mormon* contains the "fulness of the everlasting gospel"—why is this basic Mormon doctrine not mentioned or even hinted at in *The Book of Mormon*?

25   The Essentials of Salvation

What is Biblical salvation? How is it obtained? Can a person earn it through a formula of prescribed rituals and/or good works (obeying the commandments—of which there are 1,100)? Or, rather, is it a free gift, offered by a loving God to every unworthy but trusting sinner? And can a person have *assurance* of his or her salvation?

Mormons teach that Christ's death purchased

man's release from the grave, so that all people will be resurrected. So the Atonement has merely provided universal resurrection; beyond this, man must *earn* his place in one of the heavenly kingdoms. And so we read:

> We know that it is by grace we are saved, after all we can do. (2 Nephi 25:23)
>
> Grace is granted to men proportionately as they conform to the standards of personal righteousness that are part of the gospel plan. (*Mormon Doctrine*, by Bruce McConkie, p. 339)
>
> There are some who have striven to obey all the divine commandments, who have accepted the testimony of Christ, obeyed "the laws and ordinances of the gospel," and received the Holy Spirit; these are they who have overcome evil by godly works and who are therefore entitled to the highest glory. (*The Articles of Faith*, by James E. Talmage, pp. 91–92)

However, the Bible teaches:

> Now to him that worketh is the reward *not* reckoned of grace, but of debt. But to him that worketh not, but believeth in him that justifieth the ungodly, his *faith* is counted for righteousness. (Romans 4:4–5)
>
> For by grace are ye saved through *faith*; and that not of yourselves: it is the gift of God: *not* of works, lest any man should boast. (Ephesians 2:8–9)

Not by works of righteousness which *we* have done, but according to his mercy he saved us, by the washing of regeneration, and renewing of the Holy Ghost. (Titus 3:5)

How, then, do our works factor in?

For we are his workmanship, created in Christ Jesus *unto* [or, *for*] good works, which God hath before ordained that we should walk in them. (Ephesians 2:10)

This is a faithful saying, and these things I will that thou affirm constantly, that they which have believed in God might be careful to maintain good works. (Titus 3:8)

Certainly, we who are saved will desire to keep our beloved Savior's commandments and to thereby overcome the world (1 John 5:1–5). And why else should Christians do good works? So that others, seeing our godly lives—even in trying circumstances—might desire what we have and learn to love and trust our Savior. The outcome being "that we should be to the praise of his glory, [we] who first trusted in Christ" (Ephesians 1:12). "For God hath not called us unto uncleanness, but unto holiness" (1 Thessalonians 4:7). True faith in Christ will always and inevitably produce a progressively holy life.

The idea of salvation through God's grace

rather than through our own works is one of the essential beliefs of Christianity. It is also an essential part of being a Christian that one should do Christian acts; but the free salvation comes *first*, and with it the change of heart which produces the Christian life in those who accept it.

Most of us are familiar with Jesus' words in John 3:16: "For God so loved the world, that he gave his only begotten Son, that whosoever believeth in him should not perish, but have *everlasting life*." Also John 17:3: "And this is *life eternal*, that they might know thee the only true God, and Jesus Christ, whom thou hast sent." For the born-again Christian, eternal life is a *present* possession. But what do Mormon authorities say?

In their recent (2004) book *True to the Faith*, one topic covered is Salvation (pp. 150–53). We are informed that "the terms *saved* and *salvation* have various meanings." Mormon missionaries are instructed that, when asked, "Have you been saved?", "Your answer will be either 'Yes' or 'Yes, with conditions.'" Salvation, they are told, is a covenant relationship which is maintained on the basis of "obedience" to the "restored gospel" of the Mormon church.

So what about being "born again" (John 3:1–8)?

This rebirth is a process that occurs [ordinarily at the age of eight] after we have been baptized and have received the gift of the Holy Ghost. . . . You can renew that rebirth each Sabbath when you partake of the sacrament.

So it needs to be *renewed* (contrary to 2 Corinthians 5:17)! But how can any *birth* be repeatedly renewed?

And when does the "regenerated" or "saved" person receive "everlasting/eternal life"? Quite a bit later!

In the scriptures, the words *saved* and *salvation* often refer to eternal life, or exaltation. Eternal life is to know Heavenly Father and Jesus Christ and dwell with Them forever—to inherit a place in the highest degree of the celestial kingdom. To receive this great gift, we must do more than repent of our sins and be baptized and confirmed by appropriate priesthood authority. Men must receive the Melchizedek Priesthood, and all Church members must make and keep sacred covenants in the temple, including eternal marriage. [Note: Without eternal marriage to a male Mormon, women can never be exalted.]

If we use the word *salvation* to mean eternal life, none of us can say that we have been saved in mortality [i.e., while on Earth]. That glorious gift can come only after the Final Judgment.

Biblical salvation, however, is quite different—and difficult. You must first admit that you are an ungodly, wicked, corrupt, filthy, self-righteous sinner whom only the *blood of Jesus* can cleanse. Will you say, along with the Apostle Paul, right now: "I am the chief of sinners"? Only if you are willing to confess to God your complete helplessness are you a candidate for salvation; otherwise you are not!

Biblical salvation consists of three stages: First there is "regeneration" (a new birth) which is accompanied by "justification" (Romans 3:20–28, 5:1, 9). Then comes "sanctification" (John 17:17; 2 Thessalonians 2:13–15), which is spiritual growth—a lifelong fruit-producing work of the Holy Spirit who dwells within the regenerated believer. And the ultimate stage is "glorification" (Romans 8:30)—one's happy entrance into heaven! But is "eternal life" received only *then*? Or does it truly begin at the beginning? What does the Apostle John tell us?

> And this is the record, that God *hath* given to us eternal life, and this life is in his Son. *He that hath the Son hath life*; and he that hath not the Son of God hath not life. These things have I written unto you that believe on the name of the Son of God; that ye may *know* that *ye have eternal life*, and

that ye may believe on the name of the Son of God. (1 John 5:11–13)

Yes, if we are born again we already *have* eternal life, and can *know* it! Jesus Christ and His finished work is our unshakable foundation. Throughout our earthly life we merely build on *that* foundation. Our works on His behalf are like various kinds of building materials: gold, silver, precious gems—these will stand the fiery test; wood, hay, straw—these will not. So our *works* will be judged, and we shall be rewarded according to their character. But even if the "house" he has built burns up, the Christian himself is still *saved* (see 1 Corinthians 3:10–15).

QUESTION: Friend, will you not believe the above passages of Scripture and the wonderful promise of the Savior in John 5:24:

> Verily, verily, I say unto you, He that heareth my word, and believeth on him that sent me, *hath everlasting life*, and shall *not* come into condemnation; but *is passed* from death unto life.

Jesus Christ is the only trustworthy foundation! For He is the God-man, God incarnate, who is far above all angels—our High Priest, the only Mediator between God and men (see Isaiah

9:6; Philippians 2:5–11; Hebrews 1:1–13, 5:5–6; 1 Timothy 2:5). And "he was wounded for *our* transgressions [not just Adam's], he was bruised for *our* iniquities. . . . All we like sheep have gone astray; we have turned every one to his own way; and the LORD hath laid on him the iniquity of *us all*" (Isaiah 53:5–6).

So in complete *trust*, call on Him, won't you?

> For salvation that comes from trusting Christ—which is what we preach—is already within easy reach of each of us; in fact, it is as near as our own hearts and mouths. For if you tell others with your own mouth that Jesus Christ is your Lord, and believe in your own heart that God has raised him from the dead, you will be saved. For it is by believing in his heart that a man becomes right with God; and with his mouth he tells others of his faith, confirming his salvation. For the Scriptures tell us that no one who believes in Christ will ever be disappointed. (Romans 10:8–11, *The Living Bible*)

Surely, that's the *best testimony* to have. And it can be *yours*! Let Jesus be your personal Savior today. He shed His precious blood for you, personally—amazingly! Amazing grace! If you are not absolutely sure of your eternal destiny, will you not open your heart to Jesus Christ right now?

• • •

THE BIBLE SAYS:

"Every word of God is pure: He is a shield unto them that put their trust in Him. Add thou not unto His words, lest He reprove thee, and thou be found a liar." —Proverbs 30:5–6

"Heaven and earth shall pass away, but my words shall not pass away." —Matthew 24:35

"Being born again, not of corruptible seed, but of incorruptible, by the Word of God, which liveth and abideth forever. For all flesh is as grass, and all the glory of man as the flower of grass. The grass withereth, and the flower thereof falleth away: but the word of the Lord endureth forever. And this is the word which by the gospel is preached unto you." —1 Peter 1:23–25

". . . receive with meekness the engrafted word, which is able to save your souls." —James 1:21

— — — — — — — — — — —

Further information is available from:

Wilbur Lingle
6-B Swift Lane
Whiting, NJ 08759-2922
Phone: (732) 350-0735